Amanda

A LITTLE
Inspiration

Best Wishes
Diane Lewis

DIANE LEWIS

To Lou
My real life hero

ISBN-13: 978-1500168650
ISBN-10: 1500168653

Library of Congress Control Number: 2014910816
CreateSpace Independent Publishing Platform
North Charleston, South Carolina

Contents

Introduction

This book was enthusiastically put together to remind, uplift and inspire you to be all and more of who you really are.

Every day is a wonderful new journey filled with unending opportunities for joyful living and prosperity. In this classroom of life, you are learning to move forward to be your best. Some days you may fall short, whereas on other days you'll soar high above the heavens.

Remember, these are just life lessons presented to you to propel you on your path to inner greatness.

It gives me pleasure to bring to you inspirational words to encourage you, to lift you to higher vibrations, and to light your path.

Deep within your core lies your essence, where words meaningful to you resonate with joy and love.

No matter where you are, or who you have become, you soul brings to you hope and faith, attributes to keep you engaged in your quest.

It is my sincere wish that you find inspiration and guidance throughout these pages and peace within your soul.

Love to you,
Diane

Words of Inspiration

Act with kindness and the
universe will reward you.

Follow the light of your soul, and discover that the darkness holds no fears other than those which you give it.

Go within and break free from
the limits you place on yourself.

Continue to believe in the magic
you once thought was there,
it still exists.

In an endless stream there are more possibilities than one can image. Dip in and find your possibility.

Those who present challenges inspire us to seek a new level of understanding.

As you stand in the sunshine,
let the sun warm your soul
infusing you with the vibrations
that surround you.

We've all chosen our role.

Find and support the best in yourself as well as others as you intertwine and interact together.

You have the ability to turn vision into reality. Start with small visions (like planting a garden to beautify your space) and build from there. Nothing is impossible unless you think it is, but patience is key.

Failure is a way to identify what
is not currently working so that
you may overcome and conquer.

Become more than you dare to dream.

There is perfection in every
situation, deed and person.

Sometimes one must look
deeply to see it.

You are always influencing others. Make your influence compelling.

Searching is part of your journey.

It is necessary because as you
move through your searches,
your understanding expands.

Align with all those who dare to
make their dream a reality.

Let the joy of today fill your heart
and release you from the
disappointments of yesterday.

You are a branch from the
tree of life.

Like every branch you are unique
and different but also are part of
the whole.

Rejoice in who you are.

Let the flame of your soul ignite
so that you may blaze the trail of
your choosing.

Follow your path and let it lead you to where you are afraid to venture but want to go.

Live the total freedom that comes
from being your authentic self.

Clear intention, focus and desire
are the winning combinations to
success.

Waken your spirit out of its
automatic slumber and view a
whole new world waiting for
discovery.

The attributes you admire in others resides within yourself.

Break free from the mental
restraints that hold you captive.

Our bodies harbor a heart that
beats a vibration to each heart it
encounters.

Listen to the message.

Let yourself be defined by that
pivotal moment in time when you
are one with creation.

You are limitless. Let no one tell you
that you are not.

A little encouragement can
become a milestone.

The door opens for those brave
enough to wander.

Like a flower reaching for the
sun, let your heart open to feel
the richness and love of existence.

Opening yourself to new experiences expands your truth.

Ego tries desperately to be your
master at times. Realize this and
you shall overcome the barrier
that stands in your path to
greatness.

The facade that you use to shield yourself for protection only manages to block the beauty of your true being.

Don't let your fear keep you in
the shadows.

Allow the pain in your heart to be replaced by the goodness within your soul.

Let love be ever present along your path to enrichment.

Bravery has no size.
Large or small, any display of
bravery measures the same.

Diane Lewis

In every darkness there is a light
no matter how small the
glimmer.

Let the light of your soul
warm your heart.

Diane Lewis

Unseen forces surround you,
bringing you hope and courage.

Simple gestures can be gifts all in themselves.

Diane Lewis

Disappointment only occurs
when our expectations are not
met.

There is a resolution to every problem. Go quiet and trust in the divine to give you a solution.

Achieving a goal has everything
to do with belief, and nothing to
do with luck.

The fabric of your life is woven by a collection of choices intent on giving you the creative license to craft your own experience.

Your dream is simply reality not
manifested yet. Have the courage
to create it.

When you quest for something to fulfill you, it's there; you just haven't recognized it yet.

We each have a story of our life.
You choose how you wish to
relate to it.

Energy is affected by many
things, words are the most
common.

Diane Lewis

Be entwined with the positive
flow of life and let it take you to
great depths.

You will always touch someone in your path along your journey.

Time is wasted trying to please those you do not.

Diane Lewis

Make someone's day a little
brighter by being a beacon of joy.

Heroes are people we look up to
and who shape our everyday
lives. Choose to become one.

The object of asking someone's advice is to gain perspective in order to make the best choice.

Become the limitlessness
of your soul.

Always put you best foot forward,
that's all you can ask of yourself.

When you see the rays of a new day dawning, the slate of yesterday has been wiped clean and you once again can become all you are meant to be.

The qualities you admire in others can be modeled into qualities within yourself. There is no need to wish, just a desire to do.

Sometimes one must venture
alone to connect to others.

Diane Lewis

Find time to quiet your mind and
listen to the rhythm of life that
encompasses you.

It's how we behave in the face of adversity that really shows us our humanity.

Being authentic is the bravest
thing you can be.

If you do not speak when you feel injustice, then there is no blame.

To close your heart is to do a
wrong to your soul.

Our worth is measured not by others, but the value we place on ourselves.

If you truly desire change, then your actions are the way to achieve results.

Live your life with the grace of one who has the knowledge and understanding beyond this realm even if you must struggle every day to do so.

Make every day purposeful.

In the season of illumination let your soul identify with the light of the world and become the stirrings of joy for others.

Never let other people's
perceptions be your guide.

Some people look to the future
while others review the past.
Know that both begin and
end in the present.

Be the star that beckons others to
look inside themselves where
goodness resides.

To dream a dream of wisdom,
to dream a dream of valor,
is to reach beyond and impress
upon your being the dream no
more but alive.

Everyone has good intentions no matter the size, but succeeding separates the dreamer from the achiever.

Break out of the confines of your mimicry.

Time is but an element to measure. If you can get past the restrictions of your mind, you will feel freedom.

Make the story of your life
a simple one.

The power to manifest your
desire is the power to believe you
can.

A small voice can become a roar
and a belief can become a reality
if you willingly let it.

The ability to change a limiting
thought creates a new reality.

Don't suppress your spirit by
living in the shadows of
understanding.

In every corridor of life there are
pauses where a vibration pierces
the darkness and leads you to
your authentic self.

Be your essence, not your ego.

Face the light of your fears.

The greatest things you do that has the tendency to go unnoticed, is the small things you do every day.

In the contrast of life, one must
observe every view point,
understand every outcome and
be considerate to every soul.

Sometimes it takes moving out of your comfort zone, whether it be voluntary or not, to get to your soul purpose.

There's a gentle breeze to the flow
of life. Allow it to gently point you
in the direction you are meant to
go.

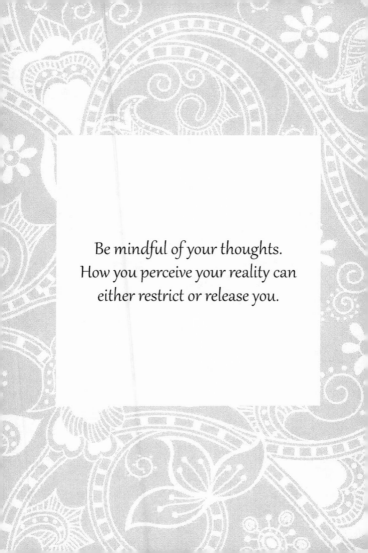

Be mindful of your thoughts.
How you perceive your reality can
either restrict or release you.

For every thought that challenges
your achievement, imagine the
possible.

You cannot possibility be enough,
you can be more.

There is a gentle breeze blowing.
Listen to the whispers in the
wind.

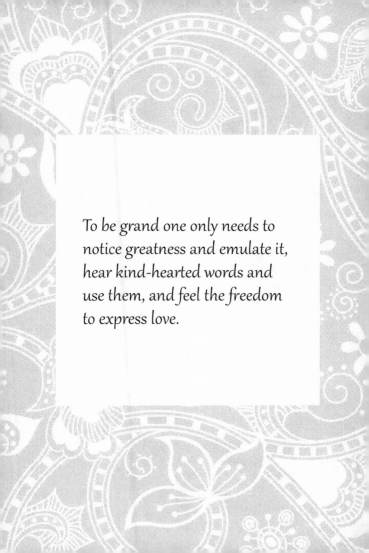

To be grand one only needs to
notice greatness and emulate it,
hear kind-hearted words and
use them, and feel the freedom
to express love.

Visualize your day from
beginning to end. Fill all your
visions with all the positive
reinforcement you need for a
successful day.

Let the joy of today fill your heart
and release you from the
disappointments of yesterday.

Never feel powerless
for every positive deed regardless
how small has far reaching
effects.

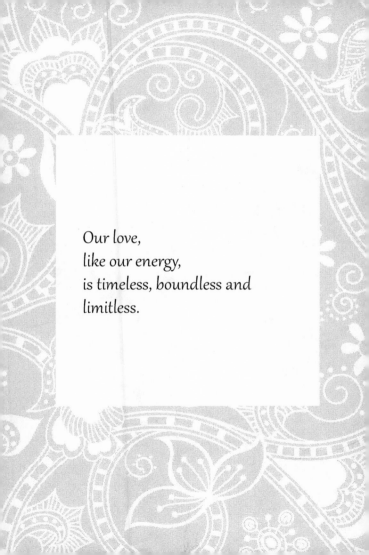

Our love,
like our energy,
is timeless, boundless and
limitless.

Ego is not our enemy; in fact it can be at times our best friend. It can propel us to achieve greater than we dared.

Knowing when it is to our benefit or not is the dilemma.

Make your own happiness your
number one priory every day.

Turn every defeat into a victory.

When you experience feelings of loneliness, it is a perception that can be changed.

All the challenges you encounter
along your path is how your
experiences are enriched with
knowledge and wisdom.

Travel lightly.

Shed the unwanted burdens that
are weighting you down on your
journey to achieve.

Regret is sorrow that another
outcome could not be achieved.

Realize that in this instance,
another outcome was never to be.

Understanding the grief in the heart of others will lead you to spontaneous kindness.

Your way to forgiving
is to simply let go.

If you want to be illuminated with insight, you must first practice to remove your focus from beyond your limited space.

Imagine your moments and
create your reality.

Bend and sway to the forces of life.
For they require a trust in the universe.

Follow the light of your heart for
it will lead you along the right
path.

Trusting in yourself and your
abilities takes courage.
The courage to leave your fears
behind.

Let it be love, desire or wanting to make your heart flutter and your soul ignite.

Loss is a state of mind.
Happiness is a state of being.
Deciding is a state of choice.

Seek the special that delights
your soul.

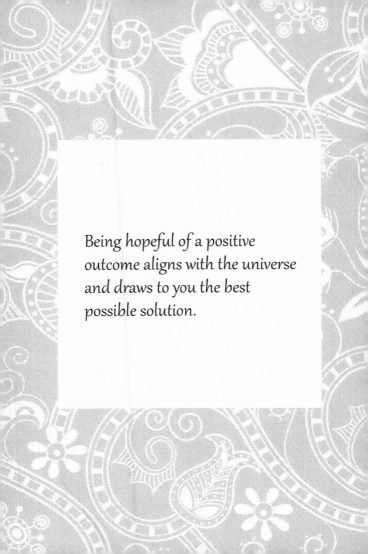

Being hopeful of a positive outcome aligns with the universe and draws to you the best possible solution.

Every emotion can become a state
of being when one chooses it as
ones intention.

If but an instant in time can set
a path intended or not, then a
choice at the crossroads becomes
the moment of truth.

Your Inner conflicts become
outer manifestations.

Take control of the conflicts
within for they are there to
strengthen you.

Simply be a light to the world.

Become the beacon to those who cannot find their way, a pillar to those whose strength is weaning and a lion to those who need the courage to be brave.

If you could see your future,
would you be quick to abandon
your today?

Creativity comes in many guises. Thinking outside the box is one of them.

Notice the little things and they will bring a ray of sunshine into your day.

Look through truthful eyes, not ones colored by the story we create in fear.

When you understand and
accept that you are more than
the sum of your humanness, do
not panic. Open yourself to the
vastness that enriches us all.

Opening the door to a new experience is a choice you give yourself to fulfill a desire of your soul.

Our emotions tell us a tale.

Listening to the wisdom
unguarded only aids the willing.

When you partner with the universe your resources are limitless.

Release any negative energy you
hold and plug in to the vibration
of life.

Reflection is a mirror of insight.

And the opportunity it affords is a chance to understand that even what you perceive as negative can have a positive effect.

Conquer your controlling
tendencies and let the rhythm of
life orchestrate the outcome.

Love will grow to be perfect if you allow it.

You have such talents but belief
needs to be one of them.

Growth comes from knowing the
difference between what was
and what is.

Find what makes you blissful
and you will discover your soul
purpose.

Be the architect of your life and create the reality of your choosing.

Diane Lewis

Quiet solitude soothes the soul,
crazy fun heals the heart.
Explore both without reservation.

138

There is a gentleness that can be felt by selflessness.

If you could tell one story of your
life, would the vibration be
positive or negative?

Time is an invaluable component of our reality.

As it passes, our moments stand as a testament to our deeds and our memories as our reminder.

Diane Lewis

Every challenge, every struggle,
every heartache and every why
you encounter brings you always
to the crossroads of choice.

At these crossroads, listen
unattended to the voice of your
soul for it will never fail to lead in
the direction of your destiny.

Since the day of your birth, you were infused with knowledge.

Everything around you beckons you to look for the clues that confirm what you had planned in this existence.

Conviction can become a tool.

Use it to overcome, to obtain, and
to be your desire.

Standing strong for yourself
encourages others to do the
same.

Get yourself in rhythm with the vibration of the universe.

The connection will inspire you in magical ways.

Gently shed what no longer suits you. Let the lesser attributes of your person fall away, leaving space to replace them with more desired qualities.

Remember: You do not have to own what you do not desire, even with self.

We are always looking in so
many directions for guidance
that we forget we only need
to look within.

When you cry in the night for the comfort of your soul, know it is your ego who weeps.

Your soul waits patiently for you to recognize the difference.

A Smile.

A marvelous design of creation to uplift a soul, recognize a kindred spirit, and feel joy from within.

A limited mindset
limits your life.

Whenever you feel doubt you
need to ascend if it came from
your heart or your head.

Planted by others speaks to your
mind, planted by spirit speaks to
your heart.

When we find an undesirable trait within ourselves blame is not the answer, change is.

For some this change may be a sprint and for others, a marathon. Regardless of which presents itself, it's about staying in the race and crossing the finish line.

Before you react to the
unexpected, take a moment and
separate from the energy. Being
thoughtful in your respond will
be more rewarding.

Separate from the fear of disappointing others and be who you really are.

Understand that on a soul level those around you are just supporting your experience.

The armor of the soul is love.

Being open depends on whether you reject what you don't want to acknowledge or accept what you dislike.

Fear can become your opponent
if you do not understand when it
is helpful and when it is not.

There is no outcome like the one you create.

Being thankful is more than words.

It is pride for all you have regardless of the amount and a feeling of contentment to the depths of your soul for all those who share in your life.

Braving the elements of your mind can sometimes be as daunting as braving a storm.

One must be diligent for changes can occur unexpectedly and elements which do not serve can engulf you quickly.

Every kind act has the capacity
to make a change, even a smile.

When looking for fulfillment you need to stand in the light of life, not the loneness of darkness.

Diane Lewis

Indulge yourself with delicious
feelings every day.

Abundance only happens when
you are open to accepting.

Reality is an illusion which changes constantly.

Desire is the cornerstone to success.

Quiet your mind and listen.

What comes to you is your
answer. Do not try to analyze it,
for once you do, you move further
from your truth and closer to
your desire.

When you get lost, turn to your internal GPS for guidance.

Light your way into tomorrow
and be a beacon of hope for
many.

Let your energy expand and comfort those around you.

Every day you choose and create
a path by your actions.

Only you can make it wonderful
journey.

When your heart is pure,
possibilities are endless.

We to often embrace the undesirable for it is the easier route.

Delight is found
when you have no expectation.

The depth of your pool of knowledge is contingent upon whether you remain safe in the shallow end.

Fear is like being on a train. Your onboard, but not in control.

Diane Lewis

Be forgiving
even in the face of disdain.

Truthful Healing is a slow process. It takes acceptance of what is and turns it into what was.

Discovering who you are
can have a profound effect
on who you become.

Have the courage to make your something happen.

Diane Lewis

Cherish your ideal.

Strength has no boundaries.

Wind it's a marvelous element of nature. This unseen force has such strength both gentle and strong, yet it's elusive.

Our soul can sometimes be like that.

Your past showers you with
memories.

Like a gentle waterfall they have
washed over you shaping you
into
the wonderful person you are.

Diane Lewis

Perspective is a funny thing, the
more you see the more it changes.

Compromise is understanding
that all views are correct.

Be determined in your quest of self and one day you may get to meet.

Every day you get another day
closer to your spiritually.

Diane Lewis

Life challenges you.
Are you ready to win?

A singing heart can be heard
around the world.

Diane Lewis

If you feel lonely, your being is
not resonating with your soul.

We all originate from the same energy regardless of our paths chosen.

Treat each soul you encounter with dignity and respect for to do so enriches your spirit.

To grow one must do more than just live. Follow your potential.

Everywhere you look there's a message. Be observant.

Influence even in the smallest
way can make a transformation.

Make your mark and
make a difference.

Your host is a temple where your
essence is housed.

There is a force that watches
allowing you the wisdom of your
own choices, but supplies the
support of your requests.

Feel powerful and when you don't, simply ask for help. It is your right to be blissful.

When you dip into the well of
knowledge you fuel your soul
with endless possibilities.

Conviction that change is already happening for your benefit is paramount to effecting change.

Diane Lewis

A moment alone is not loneliness,
It's simply a moment in time.

There is no weakness, just conviction that is lacking.

Diane Lewis

Striving is the lesson.

Resistance is just the universe's way to say look again.

It doesn't mean it not the path, but it may warrant another look to discover something unseen.

When you're asking the universe,
be patience.

Not everything is immediate. Our
celestial helpers may need some
time to orchestrate our result.

Your hopes can be realized with faith. Your faith can be realized with desire. And your desire can ignite your inner flame.

There are many treasures in life,
but those who support you
are truly invaluable.

Be divine. It only takes thinking so.

Diane Lewis

*Simple gestures of kindness
are heartfelt.*

Your energy can be felt by those
around you. Make it loving.

We are each unique in our ordinary life for we have an experience that no one else can mirror.

Sometimes what others ask of
you may be out of harmony with
yourself.

Look within and find your
courage to be exactly who you
are.

Diane Lewis

Your world expands every time
your mind opens.

When you experience
dissatisfaction,
it is an indication you have not
found the answer.

Try to remember your happy
times with the same clarity as
your hurts.

The universe lends a hand for
those who ask.

Be specific in your request as
simple is as simple does.

Diane Lewis

Questions are a learning tool.
Being afraid to ask is pure ego.

Be bold today.

Close your eyes and listen to the rhythm of life that surrounds you.

What do you hear?

Thought grants you the ability to create a new reality.

Positivity is like a river that just flows quietly in the backdrop of your life.

To break free one must resonate out of accord with an undesired vibration.

If you cannot be yourself,
become that which you desire.

Lighten your load.

Detach from a vibration that serves no purpose.

You will bend and sway through
a lifetime of challenges each
making you more unique.

Make your everyday
a bright future.

Each one of us has a gift to give.
Each one of us has a light to
share. Each one of us has a story
to tell. Each one of us is
remarkable.

About the Author

Diane Lewis is a gifted psychic medium, considered one of the best in her field. She discovered her abilities at a young age; as they matured, she sought to better understand these psychic experiences in order to further develop and refine her gifts. Today, with over twenty-five years of experience, Lewis's true talent lies in her ability to help people—connecting them with the spiritual realm and leading them to uncover their own inner greatness. She uses her gifts in private intuitive readings, medium readings, public presentations, and workshops. You can learn more about her spiritual work on her website: www.dianelewis.us.com.

Notes

Notes

Notes

Notes

_____

_____

_____

_____

_____

_____

_____

_____

_____

_____

_____

_____

_____

_____

_____

_____

_____

Notes

Notes

_____

_____

_____

_____

_____

_____

_____

_____

_____

_____

_____

_____

_____

_____

_____

Notes